Architecture Can!

Architecture Can!
Hollwich Kushner I HWKN
2008–2018

Matthias Hollwich and Marc Kushner

images
Publishing

Published in Australia in 2018 by
The Images Publishing Group Pty Ltd
ABN 89 059 734 431
The Images Publishing Group Reference Number: 1441

Offices

Australia
6 Bastow Place
Mulgrave, Victoria 3170 Australia
Tel: +61 3 9561 5544

United States
6 West 18th Street 4B
New York, NY 10011
United States
Tel: +1 212 645 1111

books@imagespublishing.com
www.imagespublishing.com

Copyright © Hollwich Kushner | HWKN 2018
The Images Publishing Group Reference Number: 1439

A catalogue record for this
book is available from the
National Library of Australia

Title: Architecture Can!: Hollwich Kushner | HWKN 2008–2018 //
Matthias Hollwich and Marc Kushner
ISBN: 9781864707915

Printed in China on 120gsm curious metallics super gold paper (pp.1–32)
and 157gsm matte art paper (pp. 33–216)

IMAGES has included on its website a page for special
notices in relation to this and its other publications.
Please visit www.imagespublishing.com

Contents

Preface

We started Hollwich Kushner in 2008 to make architecture. We did not have an agenda—just an unshakable belief in the power of buildings, an abiding love for the spaces they shape, and a naive notion that better buildings make a better world. But how?

We have pursued the answer in our work, built and unbuilt, and in this book we offer a glimpse into the projects that have furthered our search for solutions. Each project has taught us something new about the effect our buildings have on the people who encounter them. This has led to revelations about sustainability, social impact, and the power of communication, but also to subtle lessons that have accrued over time.

A decade into our joint practice, we understand

some fundamental
things about
architecture differently.
We understand that
the future is not about
designing beautiful
buildings but about
designing buildings with
personalities in order
to generate bonds with
the people who use
them. We understand
that the people who use
our buildings aren't just
the people inside, or the
people on the street, but
the global population of
consumers who clamor

for the newest images of the most advanced buildings and spaces. Finally, we understand that buildings don't just reflect our society, they shape our society.

We remain as optimistic as ever about architecture's potential to make a better world. That is why all of our work strives to empower people to engage with others, to produce memorable experiences, and to live with a sense of wonder.

This is our journey and
we look forward to
taking it with you.

—Matthias Hollwich
and Marc Kushner

Manifestos

These points encapsulate the lessons we have learned over the last ten years. They are at once observations of the innate power of architecture and goals we strive for in everything we design.

Emote

Architecture is nothing without people.

We don't believe in
a hierarchy between
inside and outside.
Our buildings are
designed to be equally
active in both realms.
Only by revealing the
pursuits within a building
and encouraging their
extension outward
can architecture be a
responsible member
of society.

Err

People aren't perfect; buildings shouldn't be, either.

We love beautiful things, but pure beauty is sterile. We don't design buildings that are flawless machines. It is the quirks and eccentricities that create character in a design, and character is eternal. Beauty fades.

Endure

Architecture lasts a really really long time.

We think about architecture as an heirloom, as something that will be used by generations of people, often people we never envisioned within our buildings. As important as it is for a building to be calibrated to its own time, it is even more important that it is capable of change.

Inspire

Architecture is a manifestation of society but does not have to reflect society.

Buildings are backdrops for life. Architects are invested with an awesome power: that of making the places where people raise their families, fall in love, turn foes into friends—and aspire toward the better.

Enable

Architecture helps people live better lives.

We don't design buildings for single moments or stages in human existence; we conceive buildings that are extensions of our physical bodies, young or old: buildings that teach us when we're young, stimulate and encourage us as we mature, and support us when our strength falters.

Unite

Buildings are the ultimate shared experience.

We design experiences that have the power to bind individuals into communities. Living in and around buildings is a universal circumstance regardless of age, creed, or orientation and thus extends opportunities to bring people together. Our buildings, rather than standing as objects of admiration, intensify the prospect of generating new bonds between people.

Disappear

Good architecture stands out. Better architecture recedes into its surroundings.

We consider it part
of our job to suss
out the exceptional
characteristics of a
site and then to infuse
our designs with those
magic ingredients. Call it
localism, or regionalism,
or whatever. To us, it is
essential that buildings
are animated by what
is near.

Insist

Architecture speaks through form, and form never stops talking.

The forms of architecture
are just as legible to
the general public
as words and body
signals. The buildings
we design broadcast
a message through
their physical presence.
The rise of social-media-
empowered criticism
and photography is the
loudest megaphone
architecture has, and
with the right tools we
tie them into the story.

Love

Emotions are not just for humans.

We often fall in love—
or indifference or
hate—with the places
we spend our time.
We design a character
into every one of our
buildings because
we think it is the
unique personalities
of certain spaces that
make them lovable.
When we get it right,
architecture becomes
more than an edifice,
it becomes a friend.

Works

Skygrove

At Skygrove we wanted to see if we could express ecological ambitions strongly enough to trigger an emotional reaction from viewers—a gut punch that would provoke them to internalize the risks of climate change. A LEED plaque in a lobby was not on our agenda. Skygrove is set in a future of runaway weather events in order to scare the public into realizing how buildings— even the mighty skyscraper—will need to adapt to a warmer, wetter world. Ultimately we hoped this would make the consequences of environmental denial more tangible to viewers, embedding a kernel of thought as to how climate change would affect them.

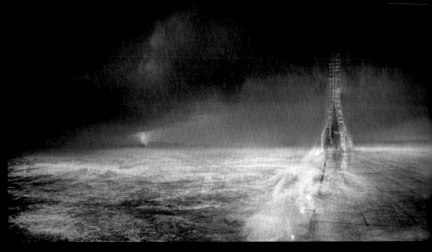

have a theory that cross-pollinating the built world and natural world awakens a sense of childlike whimsy in even the most jaded of visitors. We got to test this theory in MINI's "creative use of space" marketing campaign when we decided to see what would happen if we placed a grassy hill atop a Manhattan roof. Would an iconic natural form in an unusual setting foster a breakdown of typical behavior? The first night, when we saw a cadre of too-cool-for-school hipsters throw social caution to the wind and scramble up the hill for a game of king of the mountain, we knew that our architectural alchemy had succeeded. Fusing nature with community purpose in this way created a unique setting that invited people to look up from their phones and engage with each other. Lively concerts and dancing, serene yoga, and sincere interactions sprouted from this previously unused space high above the city.

Metreepolis

When the History Channel invited us to design Atlanta in the year 2050, we were eager to devise a solution that reached far into the speculative in order to rethink architecture, urbanism, and sustainability. The vision we developed puts humankind back in tune with nature or, more accurately, puts nature back in tune with humankind by literally manipulating it to suit human needs. At the time, MIT researchers had just harvested an electrical current from a spinach leaf. We envisioned genetically manipulated plant material becoming an active participant in providing energy for the city. The altered "power plants" fused buildings with the beauty of the natural world. Many contemporary architects and designers see themselves, and their buildings, as superior to nature; it is far more important to bring back a relationship between humans and the rest of the earth that is characterized by balance and cooperation.

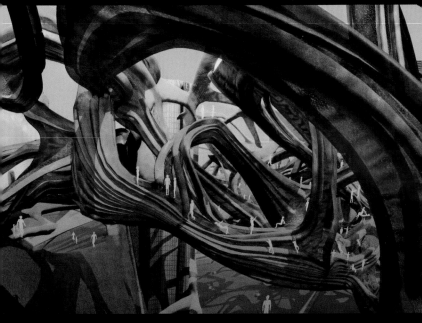

Architizer

People want to be social—so do buildings. We founded Architizer in 2008 because in the early days of social media publishing our work in architecture magazines was beginning to seem out of touch with how we were sharing information online. The platform we built hosts architectural portfolios. What we learned from the metrics—click-through rates and time-on-site—was that the public craved innovative, wildly unusual buildings. This discovery—a surprise to us—is one way social media has changed the relationship among architects, buildings, and the audience, exposing the deep seated public preference for uniqueness of place and giving architects the ultimate communications tool to speak to a global audience.

Animalation

For forty years the Black Party in New York City has brought together thousands of gay men for a night of bacchanalia. The salacious scenes that take place around the perimeter of the giant dance floor—the organizers refer to them as "curious acts"—had become so captivating that they dissipated the essential energy of the party. We wanted to see what would happen if we introduced a new focus to the space, one that would shift attention from the perimeter to the center. Since the architecture would have to compete with some very compelling content, we used mystery to draw the attention of the crowd. Our giant animated light object produced an effect similar to that of an ambiguous natural event, something like observers reading various forms into the same cloud formation. Different perceptions of the object—spider, harness, threat, refuge—created a personalized experience for each partygoer. The individual experiences, in turn, transformed passive onlookers into active participants.

Sasha Bruce House

Architecture is communal—it is one of the only experiences shared by all people of all cultures—but bringing people together to help one another is still a rarity. Nevertheless, architecture's universality can bind the most diverse crowd. That was our experience at the Sasha Bruce House, a Washington, D.C., shelter for homeless youth. Then President-Elect Barack Obama asked us—and offered to help us—to spruce up the interiors of this noble institution. The project kicked off his national call for volunteerism; even without this unique circumstance, the convergence of public-spirited individuals would have been significant.

he project involved friends, neighbors, and volunteers in a construction project that turned into a meaningful social experience for all involved. Architects have the power to include all sorts of stakeholders during the creation of a project. As we plan and construct each one, we continually ask ourselves how to build a sense of community one building at a time.

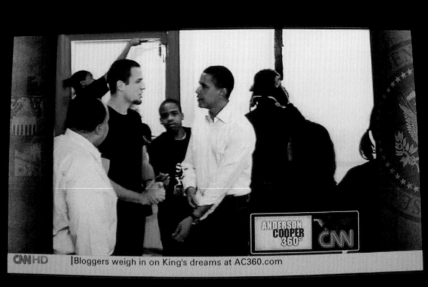

BOOM

An early client of ours motivated us to look into architecture's response to aging. What we found was shameful. Architecture does not engage with the older members of our society. In the United States, most of the responsibility for seniors' well-being has been transferred to corporations. The result is retirement communities, assisted-living facilities, and nursing homes that prevent older people from participating in the vibrancy of life. To offer some alternatives to this state of affairs, we invited ten forward-thinking architects to explore the future of aging and architecture; together, we came up with new ideas for reintegrating society's elders into the broader community. If architects work more actively to embrace older people, all ages will benefit—making all ages

able to live a desired life to the very end.

Journal Squared

We teamed up with Handel Architects on a competition for a giant residential commission in New Jersey. And we won! Since it was by far our biggest and tallest project, we wanted to do more than design for the skyline. We wanted the three-tower development to engage occupants, neighbors, users across the region, and the daily throng of drivers on the New Jersey Turnpike. We used the typical building height and width of nearby areas to derive the simple geometries. As the buildings rise, these geometries are interrupted by large cuts that extend the scale of the front door to the scale of he region. It is a way to say "Here is the front door. Please come on in," a welcome mat that's sized to the New York metropolitan region. The fifty-three-story tower—phase one—is completed and occupied; its sixty-three- and seventy-one-story neighbors constitute phases two and three.

UNIQLO Cubes

It was when we were designing one of our smallest projects that we realized social media can amplify the message of a design exponentially—physical size doesn't really matter. A nine-foot-cube can have the impact of a much larger object when every detail is geared toward an immersive experience for the user. The two temporary cubes we created for UNIQLO unite form, structure, and materiality to create a singular overwhelming effect. Gridded interior shelving at once supports the cubes, organizes the goods on sale, and epitomizes the UNIQLO aesthetic. We also applied this grid pattern onto the site itself—a plaza near New York's High Line—and shaped a public skating rink by swirling the otherwise perfect geometry of the pattern. We have found that designing pop-ups offers an opportunity to conduct high-speed architectural experiments on how architecture engages with both its environment and the people experiencing it.

Wendy

When we built Wendy for MoMA PS1, we didn't strive for perfection—we strove for lovability. Wendy is rough by design. Her roughness makes her approachable and easy to engage with. It took more than a hundred design explorations to find her spiky blue form, which maximizes surface area. This generous surface, via a coating of titanium nanoparticles, removes from the air an amount of pollution equivalent to that produced by 260 cars. Wendy created an atmosphere all her own—in addition to improving the air nearby, she spit water into the air, provided cooling shade, and let people touch, sit, hang out, and be themselves. The rented scaffolding system with which we surrounded her evocative form—a system familiar to any city dweller—eliminated any preciousness and turned Wendy into a friend—a slightly dirty, somewhat disheveled, completely lovable friend. It quickly became apparent that Wendy was a new type of social architecture.

76

Pines Pavilion

The Pines Pavilion is without question an extrovert. We didn't just deploy a litany of architectural moves to make sure visitors have a great time; we also wanted the building to broadcast these efforts by means of a strong graphic language. In this way, users would understand how hard the building was working to make their experiences memorable. The pavilion is the first structure that weekenders see when the ferry pulls up to Fire Island. Central to our design is a huge truss that frames the building's activities. When the building is empty, the facade is a welcoming icon. When it is fully occupied, the facade disappears as the buzzy party scene becomes the focal point. Smaller maneuvers, like a triangulated bar bleachers surrounding the dance floor, a bench where the building front meets the ground, and a provocatively social bathroom, give all visitors a chance to find the perfect spot to survey or partake in the scene.

JAMD Master Plan

By the time we started working on a master plan for the Jerusalem Academy of Music and Dance, the organization had spent decades in a retrofitted, acoustically leaky, 1960s office building. This contributed to an intimate and casual setting where students were not intimidated by formal architecture. We wanted to preserve this attribute in JAMD's new campus. That is why the components of the new campus—concert hall, rehearsal space, lobby, and café—are centered around an unprogrammed outdoor space. The unexpected can happen in this courtyard—from an informal concert or casual flirtation to a political speech or serious talk between friends. Yet we were careful not to confuse this type of fluidity with flexibility. We dread flex space: its movable walls and modular furniture are a sure guarantee that no one will use the space with anything more than grim acceptance. Fluid space, on the other hand, can be used for many activities without requiring a change to its architectural elements.

Architects today often present proposals with the help of diagrams that try to root design in a convincing logic. To us, this is an exhausting exercise in self-rationalization. We had always wanted to go in the opposite direction: to design a willfully illogical space to replicate the relief and serendipity we feel outdoors surrounded by the haphazard forms of the natural world. And we did so for this hotel project in the gritty urban post-industrial landscape of coastal Williamsburg. Existing forms are coopted to re-create the joy of being in nature. Seemingly random objects on a rooftop space—a hill, a bar, and a tower, all draped in a rusted cloak of CorTen steel—relate through form to the relics of the Brooklyn waterfront. While the space makes no sense through the lens of logic, it is somehow just right for the strange landscape of its setting.

MAX

The magnificent crowns of the Chrysler Building, Woolworth Building, and many others distinguish the skyline of New York from that of many other cities. But these crowns are meant to be admired from afar—the designs focus on form and beauty, not people. The same is true in traditional residential towers: penthouses at the top of the building are accessible only to the few who can afford them. For MAX, a micro-housing study for the Bloomberg administration, we turned the archetype around. The crown contains all community functions, celebrating a communal and newly reestablished connection between residents. MAX addresses the social aspect of micro-housing as it compensates for the minimization of private space by providing a new kind of amenity: camaraderie.

25 Kent

We want our buildings to push people slightly out of their comfort zone, provoking a heightened sense of community; we want people to make friends in our buildings. At 25 Kent we capitalized on the well-known dictum that social areas add great value to office buildings because informal run-ins between employees increase creativity and staff satisfaction. Hallways are replaced by a public avenue that skewers the building and acts as its main circulation spine. We exposed this central hub of activity by shaving off the short sides of the facade, revealing the building's liveliness to the neighborhood. The design turns an office building into a campus where experience takes priority over traditional workplace efficiency.

CCS Bard Hessel Museum

When the executive director of the CCS Bard Hessel Museum asked us to rethink his institution, we focused on programmatic innovation, transforming the standard museum, gallery after gallery after gallery, into a museum of the future where attentive curation is part of the experience. The renovation was more surgery than architecture: we cut new windows and skylights into the existing shell and carefully sliced and reworked the existing layout to make something entirely new. Works by two artists, one living and one dead, are installed permanently. Visitors experience art by Liam Gillick and Sol LeWitt not just as art on a wall but as architectural objects and also through written material from the artists, curators, archives, and other sources. The immersive experience, which incorporates the culture of art and its historic and social influences, opens a window to a more authentic and direct museum experience.

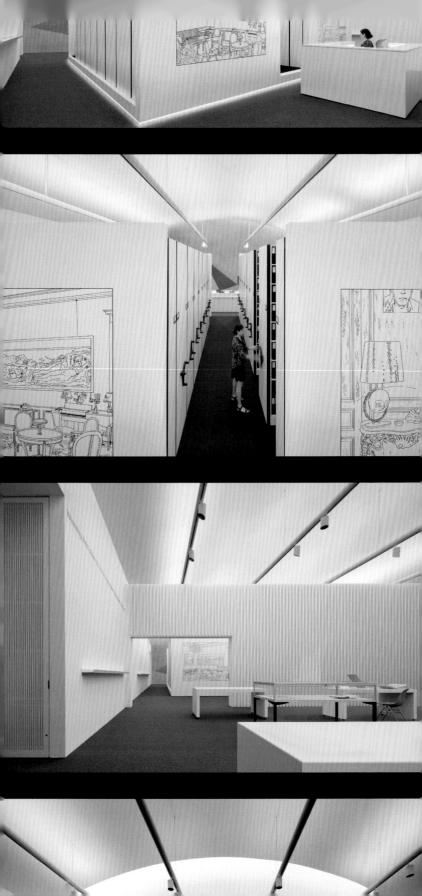

Grand Junction

We are part of the team designing a new park in Westfield, a suburb of Indianapolis. The project is designed to make the town of 37,000 into a cultural destination with a vibrant downtown, thereby preventing the decline that is affecting the nation's older suburbs. We developed four public pavilions, each a quarter of a single giant cube. Visitors to the park will experience a contrast in texture: smooth planes along the sides of the pavilions and rough surfaces on the facades cleaved from the whole. The area of communal programming—which will host concerts, picnics, ice skating, and more—is framed by the rough sides. The form(s) speak(s) to both individuality and unity, essentials in any functioning community.

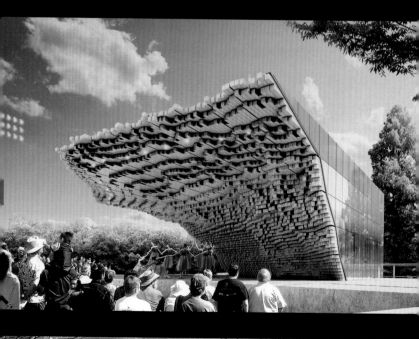

Pennovation Center

When the University of Pennsylvania invited us to transform a twentieth-century paint factory into a twenty-first-century idea factory, we contended that designed lab spaces for entrepreneurs are not enough. As the relationship between architecture and people changes to account for the value conferred on experiences (rather than on belongings), the way buildings are designed changes as well. In the past, architects have focused on program, form, materiality, and structure. All of these still matter, but precedence is now given to the way architecture empowers people to be who and what they want. To Pennovation, we added key social spaces that tempt entrepreneurs to leave their desks and engage with their colleagues. These areas are tucked into a new angular facade that reaches out toward the Schuylkill River and incorporates a bar, board room, and bleacher seating. These alluring public forums give the building the means to act as friend, mentor, partner; to have both personality and an effect on life outside its walls.

WeLive 2.0

The young adults of the 2010s—millennials—are at the forefront of a radical shift in how an individual defines him- or herself in relation to the community and the surrounding objects. Co-living, co-working, sharing, experiencing (rather than owning), and constant socializing are all part of this transformation. When WeWork hired us to rethink its WeLive product (furnished apartments with flexible lease terms) after the first iteration launched, we tapped the potential of this generation, rethinking how apartments are categorized, how people live together, and even how bedrooms, bathrooms, closets, and kitchens can be designed to best complement the intended inhabitants. Entertainment areas, amenities that rival those of vacation resorts, a sense of community that encompasses multiple dwellings—and, perhaps most important, an experimental approach—foster a truly social living experience.

Bauhaus Museum

Museums are often used to reinvigorate declining cities o
abandoned neighborhoods—but for the most part that is
outward-facing objective that is not reflected in galleries
other interior spaces. Indeed, we have observed that few
new museum buildings have radical interior reinventions.
We sought to change this in our competition entry for a
Bauhaus museum in Dessau. The proposal draws on Walt
Gropius's famed Bauhaus building but is at the same time
imbued with emotional qualities that touch visitors' hearts
In our refashioning of the museum typology, we absorbec
local traits and embedded them into the building; at the s
time we attempted to alter the form, expression, and prog
of the Gropius original. Designing a museum today is abo
inviting people to come to the city and the building. We us
this new sense of social opportunity to amplify the innova
technology, and arts of the Bauhaus.

JAMD Inter-Arts Center

In Jerusalem buildings have to be clad in Jerusalem stone. Our client warned us that most architects find this stipulation a hindrance to their designs, but we loved the challenge of engaging with a traditional local material. Our Jerusalem stone is set at a 45-degree angle in a diagrid pattern. Where the public engages with the building, at the entrance lobby and windows, for instance, we shrank the stone tiles, exposing the glass facade behind. This erosion introduces a playful quality to the facade, allowing light and air in, opening the building to its occupants, and turning a conventional building into a progressive object that acts as a social mixer for students, faculty, and visitors. In the end, the Jerusalem stone has a magical effect. The building does not compete with the city but contributes to its surroundings, complementing the urban fabric while adding its own identity to the map.

Skyler

As part of our research and design studies for New Aging (published in 2016), we developed Skyler, an architectural prototype that puts into action all the book's observations. The building exchanges traditional values of beauty for character. Dimpled and bulging, the limestone facade will streak and stain over time—as all of us will. Skyler's 1,000 inhabitants will match the population distribution by age in the United States. Thus there are 150 residents older than 65; if the building follows U.S. demographic trends, this number will double by about 2050. The tower offers a mix of micro-studios (efficient private dwellings), shared apartments (to eliminate isolation), and duplexes (single-family homes). Skyler invites people to live cooperatively, sharing facilities and services, to remain healthy, social, and active at every age. Designing through the lens of older people gives rise to strategies and solutions for ever-increasing global life expectancy. Though just a study, Skyler has inspired developers around the world to address aging.

Wharf Marina

The **Wharf Marina** floats along the Washington Channel on the edge of the new District Wharf community in Washington, D.C. At a time when most developers focus on building amenities, this building is an amenity for the entire neighborhood and the city at large, welcoming foot traffic by the water and boat traffic in the water. The building is a visual extension of a bench that edges the Washington Channel waterfront. Here the bench turns into a truss that zigzags between deck and ceiling. Housed inside of the truss is a simply detailed glass box with open interior spaces that provide uninterrupted views over the water and toward Washington's historic fabric.

New(er) York

Architecture's vibrant longevity differentiates it from the other design disciplines. Unlike painting or sculpture architecture is not preserved in a museum—it is the museum. We have often wondered why the most popular buildings in New York City were built before World War II. Beauty is fleeting, but characte is enduring, it turns out. We try to imbue our buildings with unique personalities so that they will stay vital for many years after they are built. New(er) York applies contemporary construction techniques and design methodologies to timeless New York City landmarks. We aspired to retain the visual liveliness of these buildings without directly copying their ornamentation; period details and flourishes instead inform new construction. Different cities and eras present an endless amount of inspiration—it is one of our favorite things about architecture.

Die Macherei

For our first invited competition in Europe, we synthesized
everything we had learned about architecture in New York
and applied it within a fresh context. It turned out to be the
first project where we were able to fuse an American sense of
playfulness with a European sense of community. The program   14

and we focused not on the individual structures but on creating four buildings in a considered relationship to one another. In fact, the design focused on the spaces between buildings, rather than on the buildings themselves. This focu creates tight urban corridors that offer rich and varied experiences to locals and visitors and attract urban activities to the area. Work in the twenty-first century is becoming mor of a lifestyle than a nine-to-five job. The loftlike proportions of the facades express an informality that puts people first.

Projects

001 | Skygrove | Commercial | Evolo | New York, New York
(see page 34)

002 | Takashi Murakami | Office | Kaikai Kiki New York |
Queens, New York

003 | 980 | Single-Family Apartment | Private Client | New York, New York

004 | Ecobras | Bridge | Petrobras | Rio de Janeiro, Brazil

005 | Open Theater Formiga | Cultural | Novo Horizonte | Rio de Janeiro, Brazil

006 | Bard Gallery | Cultural | Bard College | New York, New York

007 | Market Valley | Multi-Family Residential | City of Charlottesville | Charlottesville, Virginia

008 | Mauermuseum | Cultural | Senatsverwaltung für Stadtplanung | Berlin, Germany

009 | MINI Rooftop | Pop-Up | BMW MINI Brand | New York, New York (see page 36)

010 | Metreepolis | Cultural | Ideas Competition | Atlanta, Georgia (see page 39)

011 | Bauhaus Haus | Cultural | Stiftung Bauhaus Dessau | Dessau, Germany

012 | Wallunitizer | Single-Family Apartment | Private Client | New York, New York

013 | Selfless Child | Pop-Up | Lime PR | New York, New York

014 | Westkerk | Cultural | Riai | West Cork, Ireland

015 | 525 | Single-Family Apartment | Private Client | New York, New York

016 | Logarage | Garage | Private Client | Hudson, New York

017 | Architizer | Tech Start-Up | Hollwich Kushner | New York, New York (see page 40)

018 | Beirut | Cultural | Ministry of Culture, Republic of Lebanon | Beirut, Lebanon

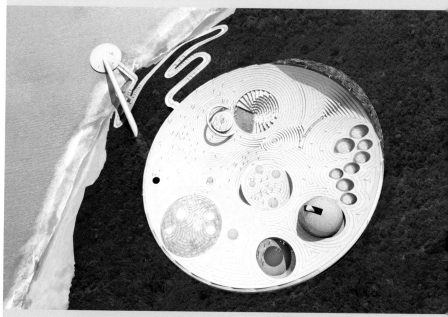

019 | Riosphere | Cultural | Arquitectum | Rio de Janeiro, Brazil

020 | Animalation | Cultural | Saint at Large | New York, New York (see page 42)

021 | Sasha Bruce House | Philanthropic | Sasha Bruce House | Washington, D.C. (see page 43)

022 | Flux Factory | Cultural | Flux Factory | Queens, New York

023 | Starz Lounge | Pop-Up | Lime PR | New York, New York

024 | Kemptnertor | Urban Landscape | Stadt Kaufbeuren | Kaufbeuren, Germany

025 | BOOM Costa del Sol | Master Plan | BOOM Communities | Malaga, Spain (see page 45)

026 | Warsaw Museum | Cultural | Museum of Polish History in Warsaw | Warsaw, Poland

027 | Space Aging | New Aging | Hollwich Kushner | New York, New York

028 | 534 | Single-Family Apartment | Private Client | New York, New York

029 | IBA 2010 | Cultural | Stiftung Bauhaus Dessau | Dessau, Germany

030 | Aging In Africa | Master Plan | Ibasho | Aby Lagoon, Ivory Coast

031 | Youth Hospital | Commercial | Baudirektion Kanton Zürich | Maennedorf, Switzerland

032 | New York 5 | Cultural | Netherlands Architecture Institute | The Netherlands

033 | Piraeus Tower | Commercial | GreekArchitects.gr | Athens, Greece

034 | HKBCF | Bridge | Highways Department | Hong Kong

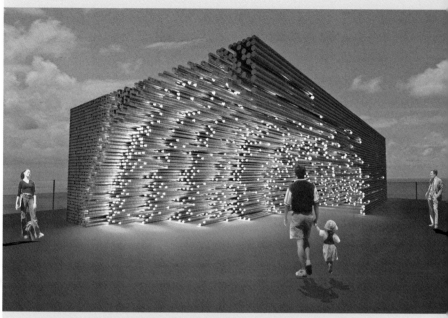

035 | Holocaust Memorial | Cultural | Atlantic City Boardwalk
Holocaust Memorial | Atlantic City, New Jersey

036 | Il Laboratorio | Retail | Il Laboratorio del Gelato |
New York, New York

037 | Turku | Cultural | City of Turku | Turku, Finland

038 | Marine Music Center | Cultural | Kaohsiung City | Kaohsiung City, Taiwan

039 | Zurich Bath | Cultural | Amt für Hochbauten, Stadt Zürich | Zurich, Switzerland

040 | Roof for Good | Philanthropic | Goods for Good | Malawi

041 | 18 Park | Multi-Family Residential | KRE Group; Ironstate | Jersey City, New Jersey

042 | Visegrád | Commercial | Hydroelectric Power Plants on Drina River | Visegrád, Czech Republic

043 | Kurhaus | Commercial | Stadt Bad Bevensen | Bad Bevensen, Germany

044 | Journal Squared | Multi-Family Residential | KRE Group; National Real Estate Advisors | Jersey City, New Jersey (see page 47)

045 | Google Lounge | Retail | Google | New York, New York

046 | Element Hotel | Hospitality | Ironstate; The Pegasus Group for Starwood Hotels | Harrison, New Jersey

047 | AOL Friends of Friends | Retail | AOL | New York, New York

048 | UNIQLO Cubes | Retail | UNIQLO | New York, New York (see page 63)

049 | Taiwan Museum | Cultural | Taipei City | Taipei, Taiwan

050 | BOOM Palm Springs | Master Plan | BOOM Communities | Palm Springs, California (see page 45)

051 | Heineken Club | Retail | Heineken | New York, New York

052 | Wendy | Cultural | MoMA PS1 | Queens, New York
(see page 76)

053 | Pines Pavilion | Cultural | Blesso Properties | Fire Island,
New York (see page 91)

054 | MenScience | Retail | MenScience | New York, New York

055 | VW Blue Motion | Retail | Volkswagen | New York, New York

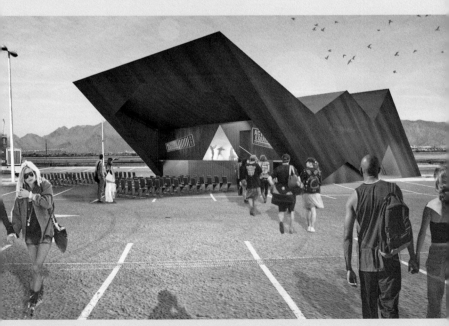

056 | Actors Equity | Pop-Up | VP+C | Mobile

057 | JAMD Master Plan | Cultural | Jerusalem Academy of Music and Dance | Jerusalem, Israel (see page 104)

058 | Jawbone Pop-Up | Retail | Weststudios | Coachella, California

059 | Wendy Abu Dhabi | Cultural | Salama bint Hamdan
Al Nahyan Foundation | Abu Dhabi, United Arab Emirates

060 | Rio House | Single-Family House | Private Client |
Rio de Janeiro, Brazil

061 | 281 Fifth Avenue | Multi-Family Residential | KRE Group | New York, New York

062 | Hotel in Williamsburg | Hospitality | Heritage Equity Partners | Brooklyn, New York (see page 107)

063 | MAX | Micro-Housing | Blesso Properties; Bronx
Pro Group | New York, New York (see page 108)

064 | DC Fishmarket | Commercial | PN Hoffman |
Washington, D.C.

065 | Chestnut Street | Multi-Family Residential | SSH Real Estate | Philadelphia, Pennsylvania

066 | Steven Alan | Retail | Steven Alan | Atlanta, Georgia; Chicago, Illinois; Dallas, Texas; Portland, Oregon

067 | Range Rover Pop-Up | Pop-Up | Jaguar Land Rover North America | New York, New York

068 | 485 Marin | Multi-Family Residential | KRE Group | Jersey City, New Jersey

069 | T'rumah | Cultural | Unscrolled | New York, New York

070 | Calvin Klein Jeans | Retail | Calvin Klein | New York, New York

071 | MoMA PS1 Roof | Cultural | MoMA PS1 | Queens, New York

072 | 25 Kent | Commercial | Heritage Equity Partners; Rubenstein Partners | Brooklyn, New York (see page 112)

073 | Au Bon Pain | Retail Prototype | Au Bon Pain | Brooklyn, New York

074 | Knightsbridge | Retail | Knightsbridge | New York, New York

075 | Ming and Mei | Cultural | Taichung City Cultural Center | Taichung, Taiwan

076 | Press 9 | Single-Family House | Private Client | New York, New York

077 | Botel | Commercial | Blesso Properties | Fire Island, New York

078 | Brooklyn Library | Cultural | Brooklyn Public Library | Brooklyn, New York

079 | Blesso House | Single-Family House | Blesso Properties | Powder Mountain, Utah

080 | Fekkai | Retail | Fekkai | New York, New York

081 | Atlantic Center | Multi-Family Residential | Forest City Ratner | Brooklyn, New York

082 | TXL | Master Plan | Land Berlin | Berlin, Germany

083 | Zaldy HQ | Office | Zaldy | New York, New York

084 | CCS Bard Hessel Museum | Cultural | Bard College | Annandale-on-Hudson, New York (see page 113)

085 | Normal | Retail and Office | Normal | New York, New York

086 | MRHS | New Aging | Morningside Retirement and Health Services | New York, New York

087 | Bayonne | Mixed-Use | KRE Group | Bayonne, New Jersey

088 | BNDES | Commercial | BNDES | Rio de Janeiro, Brazil

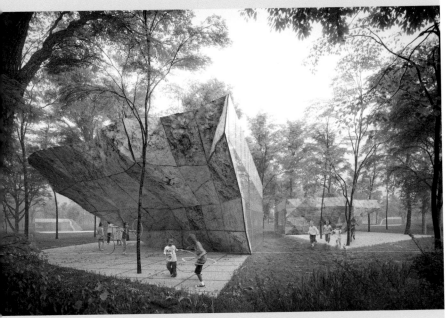

089 | Grand Junction | Cultural | City of Westfield | Westfield, Indiana (see page 115)

090 | Quirky SF | Office | Quirky | San Francisco, California

091 | Pennovation Center | Institutional | University of
Pennsylvania | Philadelphia, Pennsylvania (see page 117)

092 | Guggenheim Helsinki | Cultural | Guggenheim Museum |
Helsinki, Finland

093 | Block 5 | Multi-Family Residential | KRE Group | Jersey City, New Jersey

094 | Second Avenue | Mixed-Use | KRE Group | New York, New York

095 | Flushing | Commercial | BronxPro | Queens, New York

096 | Building 4 | Multi-Family Residential | Ironstate | Harrison, New Jersey

097 | NYC ACC | Pop-Up | NYC ACC | New York, New York

098 | Calvin Klein | Retail | Calvin Klein | New York, New York

099 | JFK Airport | Master Plan | Port Authority of New York and New Jersey | New York, New York

100 | Crystal City Plaza 5 | Multi-Family Residential | Vornado/ Charles E. Smith | Arlington, Virginia

101 | TWC Pavilions | Pop-Up | Related | New York, New York

**102 | WeLive 2.0 | Multi-Family Residential | WeWork |
Worldwide (see page 132)**

CONFIDENTIAL

103 | WeLive Prototypes | Residential Prototype | WeWork |
New York, New York

104 | Bauhaus Museum | Cultural | Bauhaus Foundation
Dessau | Dessau, Germany (see page 133)

105 | WeLive Miami | Multi-Family Residential | WeWork | Miami, Florida

106 | 39 Park | Single-Family House Private Client | Long Branch, New Jersey

107 | Market Square | Mixed-Use | Wexford Science + Technology | Philadelphia, Pennsylvania

108 | 2121 | Commercial | Vornado | Crystal City, Virginia

109 | JAMD Inter-Arts Center | Cultural | Jerusalem Academy of Music and Dance | Jerusalem, Israel (see page 135)

110 | Fire Island Arts Center | Cultural | BOFFO | Fire Island, New York

111 | Amagansett Residence | Single-Family House | Private Client | Amagansett, New York

112 | Yards Hotel | Hospitality | PN Hoffman | Washington, D.C.

113 | Buzzard Point | Master Plan | Akridge | Washington, D.C.

114 | Skyler | Mixed-Use, New Aging | Hollwich Kushner | Speculative Site (see page 137)

115 | King Street | Multi-Family Residential | Toll Brothers |
New York, New York

116 | MALI Museum | Cultural | Lima Art Museum | Lima, Peru

117 | Wharf Marina | Retail | PN Hoffman; Madison Marquette | Washington, D.C. (see page 139)

118 | Casper Sleep Shop | Retail | Casper | New York, New York

119 | Science Island | Cultural | Kaunas City Municipality | Kaunas, Lithuania

120 | New(er) York | Design Research | Hollwich Kushner | New York, New York (see page 141)

121 | Die Macherei | Office and Hospitality | Art Invest Real Estate; Immobilien | Munich, Germany (see page 144)

122 | Warsaw Bridge | Bridge | City of Warsaw | Warsaw, Poland

123 | Pier One | Commercial | DS Bauconcept | Düsseldorf, Germany

124 | 378 Broome Street | Multi-Family Residential | Urban Standard Development | New York, New York

125 | Elbtower | Mixed-Use | HafenCity Hamburg | Hamburg, Germany

Acknowledgments

Special thanks to my family: Barbara Hollwich, Walter Hollwich, Trixi Hollwich, Charlotte (Omi) Hollwich, Anna (Mausi) Streb-Lorey, Uschi Stieger, James Roebuck, Michael McElroy, Chris Session, Cornel Van West, Arnold Thielman, Marcel Horne

Teachers: Frau Braun, Frau Schneider, Frau Klein-Lauw, Herr Baeumler, Heike Buettner

Friends and collaborators: Anna Klingmann, Filip Noterdaeme, Bruce Fisher, Marc Rosa, Paul Lewis, Matthijs Bouw, Rainer Weisbach, Dietmar Starke, Jürgen Mayer H., Alexander Diehl, Hunter Tura, Kitty Leering, Benjamin Prosky, Hunter Tura, Patrick Nolan

Key co-workers: Joshua Prince-Ramus, Wilfried Hackenbroich, Sarah Dunn, Fernando Romero, Dan Wood, Bjarke Ingels, Ole Scheeren, Minsuk Cho, Floris Alkemade, Gary Bates

Employers and mentors: Wolfi Kornemann, Roy Gelders, Liz Diller, Ricardo Scofidio, Peter Eisenman, Rem Koolhaas, Gregory Clement, Aaron Tan, Marc Angélil, Omar Akbar, Detlef Mertins, Marilyn Jordan Taylor, Dr. William W. Braham, Gary Handel

And the best business partner ever: Marc Kushner.

—Matthias

Thanks to Chris Barley, Matthias Hollwich, and my family, friends, and colleagues for your years of support.

—Marc

This book would not be possible without the support of our clients: Marcia Acita, Omar Akbar, Steven Alan, Kenneth Alexander, Her Highness Sheikha Salama bint Hamdan Al Nahyan, Abdallah Al Shami, Faris Al-Shathir, Gretchen Awalt, Andrew Bank, Gabe Banner, Dave Barry, Steven Becker, Barry Bergdoll, Klaus Biesenbach, Matt Blesso, Steve Blum, Mitch Bonanno, Ron Bruno, Ann Butler, Noah Chrismer, Mayor Andy Cook, Edwin Datz, Kevin Davis, Garland DeGraffenried, Markus Diegelmann, Tom Eccles, Michael Ellch, Andreas Eule, Maria Feicht, Frederic Fekkai, Nate Fishkin, Will Fleissig, Gordon Fraley, Tom Gough, Louis Greco, Tony Greenberg, Amy Gutmann, Craig Harwood, David Hilde, Monti Hoffman, David Hollenberg, Joseph Jewell, John Scott Johnson, Melody Jones, Jeffrey Kanne, Jeremy Kaplan, Robert Kasirer, Ben Kaufman, Nikki Kaufman, Charlie Kehler, Andrew Kirtzman, Valerie Klos, Mark Kocent, Alain Kodsi, Andreas Krause, Guenter Krause, Gaia Krauss, Jourdan Krauss, Michael Krog, Stefan Kronenberg, JP Kuehlwein, Jon Kushner, Kim Kushner, Lee Kushner, Melissa Kushner, Murray Kushner, Taryn Laeben, Rob Lalumia, Yinam Leef, Evan Regan Levine, Michael Lichtenstein, Kathy Listermann, Glenn D. Lowry, Jeffrey Lui, Nicole Macaluso, Samantha Magistro, Raoul Mambo, Miguel McKelvey, Andrew Miller, Toby Millman, Eleanor Morgan, Toby Moskovits, Takashi Murakami, Adam Neumann, Paul Nikolaidis, Meir Nitzan, Patrick Nolan, Anne Papageorge, Kari Parekh, Neil Parikh, Esther Perman, Jeff Persky, Stephen Pevner, Mike Pfeffer, Claudette Pohl, Tracy Pollock, Adam Press, Guido Prummer, Joe Punia, Roni Rahar, Bruce Ratner, Joseph Reagan, Peter Reed, Jamie Ronga, Philip Rosenzweig, Steven Roth, David Rubin, Federico Sanchez, Tim Saternow, Mitchell Schear, Bob Schofield, Laura Schonfeld, Illan Schul, Michael Schüßler, Richard Sciaretta, Shawn Seaman, Jason Segal, Paul Sehnert, Luke Sherwin, Elinor Shram, Henry Smedley, Kristi Smith, Jon Snyder, Pete Soens, Paul Sowter, Ferdinand Spies, Stefan Stadler, Dietmar Starke, Matthew Steenhoek, Jens Stenzel, Joshua Sternberg, Maximilian Stier, Paul Stovall, Claudia Struss, Steven Swanson, Mithat Tal, Chen Tamir, Julia Telzak, Ann Thompson, Pete Trentacost, Mark Veeder, David Von Spreckelsen, Todd Waterbury, Seth Weisman, Dieter Weiss, Tobias Wilhelm, Fred Wilson, Joanne Wilson, Heather Wischmann, Andre Wollny, Josh Wuestneck, Mary Yagi, Fuaud Yasin, Thomas Yoo

Firm Profile

Hollwich Kushner is a leading architecture firm based in Lower Manhattan and winners of the prestigious MoMA/PS1 Young Architects Program where they built Wendy. The firm has gone on to design projects at every scale: intimate to awe-inspiring, and everything in-between. Hollwich Kushner creates forward-looking buildings that place people first. They are a new kind of architecture firm that believes in entrepreneurship—they founded Architizer.com and were named one the world's Most Innovative Companies by Fast Company.

Matthias Hollwich, AIA, has established himself at the forefront of a new generation of groundbreaking international architects. A co-founder of Architizer, Matthias believes the key to successful architecture lies in finding new and exciting ways to create dialogue and relationships between people and buildings. He was recently named in Business Insider's list of top business visionaries, has spoken regularly at events, such as TED and PICNIC, and has taught architecture as a visiting Professor at the University of Pennsylvania. Alongside his work with Hollwich Kushner, Matthias is a thought leader on the topic of "new aging" having developed a number of architectural opportunities and strategies to better accommodate our aging populations, the latter of which are featured in Matthias' second title *New Aging: Live Smarter Now to Live Better Forever*.

Marc Kushner, AIA, is an architect with just one agenda: he wants you to love architecture. As partner at Hollwich Kushner and co-founder and CEO of Architizer, Marc is a celebrated designer and pioneer in the digital media industry. Marc presents at events such as TED, PSFK, and GRID on topics surrounding architecture's intersection with digital media. He is the 2017 Harvard Graduate School of Design Entrepreneur in Residence and has taught at Columbia University's GSAPP. His book *The Future of Architecture in 100 Buildings* is ranked in the top ten in Architecture on Amazon. Marc is also the President of the Board of Friends of + POOL, a nonprofit behind the development of a water-filtering, floating swimming pool that will filter and clean urban rivers.

Team

Tim Aarsen, Jamie Abrego, Zack Aders, Anwar Alkhatib, Amanda Azzahra, Victor Barbalato, Chris Barley, Dorin Baul, Sejal Bhimjiani, Yuval Borochov, Andreas Bottler, Kathleen Cayetano, Joshua Chan, Franco Chen, Ja-Sheng Chen, Terri Chiao, Matt Choot, Egbert Miles Chu, Maru Chung, Brandon Conde, Jared Culp, Jaime Darrow, Kyle Del Vecchio, Joseph Di Matteo, Jordan Doane, Ryan Donaghy, Daniel Elmore, Dwight Engel, Brad Engelsman, Nicole Estevez, Lindsay Farrell, Peter Feigenbaum, Ana Ferrel, Jerry Figurski, Evan Fox, Jefferson Frost, Will Fu, Daniel Gaertner, Tina Gao, Tanya Gershon, Daniel Gillen, Michael Francis Golden, Alana Goldweit, Jared Greenman, Keith Greenwald, Joel Hagerty, Myriam Hamdi, Patrick Herron, Alberto Herzog, Matthew Hoffman, Adam Hostetler, Cynthia Hsu, Nicole Huang, Carlos Jadraque, Soon Jae Kwon, Elisabeth Jessenitschnig, Ignas Kalinuska, Matthew Kaltman, John-Thaddeus Keeley, Benedikt Kellner, Will Kemper, Amy Kessler, Timothy Khalifa, Dongil Kim, Joan Kim, Juhyun Kim, Taehee Joan Kim, Taesoo Kim, Jessica Knobloch, Louis Koehl, Andreas Kostopoulos, Jonathan Kowalkoski, Joseph Kuhn, Marilin Laenen, Justin Lai, Kim Lai, Rohita Land, Vittoria Le Donne, Chung-Wei Lee, David Lee, Hwaseop Lee, Nicolas Lee, Parker Lee, Wes LeForce, Kelsey Lents, Joelle Lichtman, Evan Litvin, Edwin Liu, Benjamin Loiseau, Cameron Longyear, Alda Ly, Robert May, Andrew McBride, Sam McCubbin, Micah McKelvey, Valentina Mele, Virginia Melnyk, Marcel Mercado, Scott Miller, Konstantin Molodovsky, Ben Muller, Greg Nakata, Corliss Ng, TJ O'Keefe, Tom Orton, Eun Sun Park, Mark Paz, Marc Perrotta, Nora Peyer, Gregory Pietrycha, Shun Ping Liu, Joanne Pouzenc, Emily Puhnaty, Clare Reidy, Brian Richter, Sebastian Rodriguez, Lindsay Rule, Martin Safar, Patricia Sahm, Paul Sanders, Alexander Sassaroli, Valentin Schmidhuber, Kate Scott, Daniel Selenksy, Todd Shapiro, Jim Shi, Tony Shi, Woo-Young Shim, Matthew Shulman, Koren Sin, Gagandeep Singh, Phillip Song, Caitlin Swaim, Cynthia Tang, Andreas Tjeldflaat, Alex Tseng, Kate Van Nelson, Ife Vanable, Jason Vereschak, Janine Vero, Lily Wan, Nathan Wang, Ian Watchorn, Evan Watts, Jessica Wetters, Brett Wiemann, Agnieszka Wojciechowicz, Karen Wong, Anna Wu, Laura Yang, Malika Yapa, Robert Yoos, Kuai Yu, Axelle Zemouli, Fan Zhang

Architecture Can! Hollwich Kushner | HWKN 2008–2018

Authors: Matthias Hollwich and Marc Kushner
Editor: Andrea Monfried
Graphic Designer: Paul Ouwerkerk
Project Director: Kim Lai
Project Manager: Emily Puhnaty
Text Editor: Gina Tsarouhas
Production Manager: Nicole Boehringer
Contributing Writer: Jennifer Krichels
Principal Photographer: Michael Moran